COCKTAIL'S

Premium Quality Goods

First published in may 2020 by,

The Leaf Books

TEL: +44(07599871195)

EMAIL:THELEAFBOOKS@OUTLOOK.COM

Cocktail

A cocktail is an alcoholic mixed drink, which is either a combination of spirits, or one or more spirits mixed with other ingredients such as fruit juice, flavoured syrup, or cream. There are various types of cocktails, based on the number and kind of ingredients added.

DRINK RESPONSIBLY

Content

Classic Cocktails

Apple Martini

Ingredients

1 1/2 Ounces Vodka

1 Ounce green apple schnapps

1/4 Ounce lemon juice

Preparation

Pour all of the ingredients into a shaker with ice and shake well.

Strain into a chilled cocktail glass.

Pina Colada

Ingredients

120ml. Pineapple juice

45ml White Rum

30ml Coconut cream

2 cups crushed ice

Preparation

pour all of the ingredients into a blender. Blend briefly at high speed.

Strain into a glass and serve

Garnish with a slice of fresh Pineapple and a cherry

Mojito
Ingredients

1.25 Ounce spiced Rum

12 Mint leaves

1 tbsp Sugar

0.5 Ounce Lime juice

2 Ounce.Soda

Preparation

Mint sprigs muddled with sugar and lime juice. Rum added and topped with soda water. Garnished with mint leaves. Served with a straw

Sea Breeze

Ingredients

4 Ounce Cranberry juice

1.75 Vodka

1 Ounce Grapefruit juice

Preparation

Pour all ingredients into a highball glass filled with ice. Garnish with lime wedge.

Manhattan

Ingredients

1 Ounce Scotch Whisky

0.5 Ounce Sweet Vermouth

Cherry

Preparation

Stirred over ice , strained into a chilled cocktail glass, Garnished with cherry and served straight up.

Margarita

Ingredients

1 1/2 Ounce Tequila

1/2 Ounce triple sec

1 Ounce lemon juice

Salt

Preparation

Pour all ingredients into a shaker with ice. Shake well and strain into a cocktail glass rimmed with salt.

Cosmopolitan

Ingredients

1.25 Ounce Vodka

0.25 Ounce triple sec

1 Ounce Cranberry juice

1 lemon twist

Preparation

Pour all ingredients into a cocktail shaker filled with ice .
Shake well and strain into a cocktail glass. Garnish with lemon twist. Served straight up without ice.

Strawberry Daiquiri

Ingredients

Strawberries
1 fresh lime
1 Cup of Ice
1 Ounce Rum
Mint leaves

Preparation

pour all of the ingredients into a
blender. Blend briefly at high speed.
Pour into a tall glass .
Garnish with mint leaves

Sex On the Beach

Ingredients

25 ml Ounce Vodka

20 ml Cranberry juice

25 ml peach Schnapps

40 ml Orange juice

Orange / Lemon slice

Preparation

Pour all ingredients into a cocktail shaker.

Shake well.

Pour into a highball glass filled with ice.

Garnish with Orange/Lemon slice.

Tequila Sunrise
Ingredients

3 Ounce (6 parts) Orange juice
1 1/2 Ounce (3 parts) Tequila
1/2 Ounce (1 part) Grenadine syrup

Preparation

Pour the Tequila and Orange juice into glass over ice. Add the Grenadine, which will sink to the bottom. Do not stir. Garnish and serve

Bloody Mary

Ingredients

4.5 cl (3 parts) Vodka
9 cl (6parts) Tomato juice
1.5 cl (1 part) Lemon juice
2 to 3 dashes of Worcestershire sauce
2 to 3 dashes of Tabasco sauce
pinch of Salt
pinch of Black pepper

Preparation

Stirring gently, Pour all
ingredients into a highball
glass.
Garnish and serve

Vodka Martini

Ingredients

6 cl (6 parts) Vodka
1 cl (1 part) dry Vermouth
lemon peel/ Olive

Preparation

Pour all ingredients into a mixing glass with ice. Shake well. Strain into a chilled cocktail glass. Squeeze oil from lemon peel onto the drink or garnish with a olive.

Mai Tai

Ingredients

1 1/2 Ounce White Rum

3/4 Ounce Dark Rum

1/2 Ounce fresh Lime juice

1/2 Ounce Orange Curacao

1/2 Ounce Orgeat syrup

Preparation

Shake all ingredients except the Dark Rum together in a mixer with ice. Strain into highball glass and float Dark Rum onto the top. Garnish and serve with a straw. Served on the rocks, Poured over ice.

Long Island Iced Tea

Ingredients

1/2 Ounce Vodka

1/2 White Rum

1 Ounce Lemon juice

1/2 Ounce Tequila

1/2 Ounce Triple sec

splash of Cola

Sliced Lemon

Preparation

Add all ingredients into a highball glass filled with ice. Stir gently. Garnish with a slice of lemon and serve with a straw.

Champagne Cocktail

Ingredients

1/3 Ounce Cognac

3 Ounce Champagne

2 Dashes Angostura bitters

1 sugar cube

Preparation

Add dash of Angostura bitter onto sugar cube and drop it into a champagne flute. Add Cognac followed by gently pouring chilled Champagne. Garnish with Orange slice or cherry.

AZ's
Cocktail Twists

Originality

Hawaiian Sunset

Ingredients

1 (part) Vodka
1 (part) White Rum
40 cl Orange Curacao
20 cl Mango juice
Ice

Preparation

Pour Mango juice in highball glass filled with ice, Then add the White Rum and Vodka followed by the Orange Curacao. Stir gently.Garnish and serve

Ibiza Rocks

Ingredients

3 (parts) Vodka
1 (part) Orange juice
1 (part) Lemon juice
Orange slices

Preparation

Pour all the ingredients into a shaker and shake well.now strain into a glass.garnish with Orange slice and serve

California Sherbet

Ingredients

2 (parts) White Rum
1 (part) Dark Rum
1 (part) Cranberry juice
1 (part) Orange Curacao
cherry / Orange slice
ice

Preparation

pour all of the ingredients into a blender. Blend briefly at high speed. Pour into a tall glass . Garnish with Orange slice and Cherry.

Shooting Star

Ingredients

3 (parts) White Rum
1 (part) Lychee juice
1 (part) Raspberry juice
Mint leaves/Raspberry

Preparation

pour all of the ingredients into a blender. Blend briefly at high speed. Pour into a tall glass . Garnish with mint leaves and Raspberry. Serve.

Mango Crush

Ingredients

1 (part) White Rum
1 (part) vodka
2 (parts) Mango juice
Diced Mango

Preparation

pour all of the ingredients into a blender. Blend briefly at high speed. Pour into a tall glass .
Garnish with mint leaves

Tropical Havana

Ingredients

2 (parts) White Rum

1 (part) Dark Rum

2 (parts) Coconut Water

Orange / Lemon Slices

Strawberries/ Raspberries

Blackberries

Mint leaves

Preparation

Add all ingredients into a highball glass filled with ice. Stir gently. Garnish with a slice of lemon / Lime and Mint leaves, Then serve with a straw.

Cuban Punch

Ingredients

3 (parts) White Rum
1 (part) Grapefruit juice
1 (part) Pineapple juice
Orange Slice

Preparation

Add all ingredients into a cocktail glass filled with ice. Stir gently. Garnish with a slice of Orange and serve.

Orange Passion

Ingredients

2 (parts) Vodka
1 (part) Orange Curacao
1 (part) Prosecco
1 (part) Bucksfizz
1 part Orange juice
Ice

Preparation

pour all of the ingredients into a
blender. Blend briefly at high speed.
Pour into a tall glass .
Garnish with mint leaves

Mocktails

Non Alcoholic beverages

A mixture of Fruit juices or Soft drinks.

San Francisco

Ingredients

60 ml Freshly squeezed Orange juice
60 ml Del Monte Pineapple juice
60 ml peach juice
60 ml Freshly squeezed lemon juice
5 ml Pomegranate syrup
Orange slice / Cherry

Preparation

Pour all ingredients over ice cubes in a chilled glass and stir. Garnish with Orange slice or cherry.

Pina Colada

Ingredients

3 (parts) Pineapple juice
1 (part) cream soda
1 (part) Coconut milk / Cream
ice
Pineapple Wedge

Preparation

pour all of the ingredients into a blender. Blend briefly at high speed.
Pour into a glass .
Garnish with Pineapple wedge.

Shirley Temple

Ingredients

Splash of grenadine syrup
Glass of Ginger ale
slice of Lemon
Maraschino Cherry

Preparation

Add a splash of Grenadine to a glass of Ginger ale. Garnish with a Lemon slice or cherry.

Roy Rogers

Ingredients

Splash of Grenadine syrup
Glass of Cola
Maraschino Cherry

Preparation

Add a splash of Grenadine to a glass of Cola, Garnish with a maraschino cherry.

Pink Lemonade

Ingredients

3 Ounce (parts) Lemonade
4 Ounce (parts) Raspberries
Slice of Lemon
Ice

Preparation

pour all of the ingredients into a blender. Blend briefly at high speed.
Pour into a glass .
Garnish with Lemon slice.

Tropical Fizz

Ingredients

5 Strawberries
1 Kiwi fruit, peeled and chopped
2 Pineapple rings,
1 (part) Sparkling apple juice
1 (part) Tropical fruit juice
1 (part) Soda water
Kiwi slice

Preparation

pour all of the ingredients into a
blender. Blend briefly at high speed.
Pour into a glass .
Garnish with Kiwi slice.

Raspberry Lemonade Slush

Ingredients

10 Raspberries
1 glass of Lemonade
ice
Cherry and Orange slice

Preparation

pour all of the ingredients into a blender. Blending at high speed. Pour into a glass .
Garnish with a cherry and Orange slice.

New Year Sunrise

Ingredients

3 (parts) Orange juice
1 (part) Lemonade
1/2 (part) Grenadine
Orange slice

Preparation

First add the Orange juice to a highball glass, Then the Lemonade followed by the Grenadine poured slowly. Garnish with Orange slice.

Summer Days

Ingredients

1 (part) Sparkling water
1 (part) Tropical juice
2 (parts) Pineapple juice
Lime slice

Preparation

Pour all ingredients over ice cubes in a chilled glass and stir. Garnish with Orange slice or cherry.

The Leaf Books

READING AT IT'S BEST !

Produced and edited by A.Fairall

Thank you for reading !

Printed in Great Britain
by Amazon

35517032R00025